Stock Markets for Fun, Profit, Self Employment and Beginners

As Taught at Western Colorado Community College

This book is not intended to give tax or legal advice, and should not be construed to be doing so. Please consult a tax and legal professional before making decisions that may have legal and tax implications.

© 2023
by Aaron Brachfeld
ISBN: 9798375643922

Table of Contents

Chapter 1: Introduction to the Stock Markets — 6
    History of Stock and Exchanging Stock — 7
    Selling Stock Requires Monetization — 7
    Valuation of Money — 8
    When Stock Prices are Anticipatory: Bull and Bear Markets — 9
    When Stock Prices are Reactionary — 10
    The Stock Market — 11

Chapter 2: Introduction to Auctions — 16
    Swapping and Trading — 17
    Price Tags — 18
    English or Forward Auction — 18
    Dutch or Reverse Auction — 20
    Japanese Auction — 21
    Timed Auction — 22
    Free Market Behavior — 22

Chapter 3: Basics of Predation — 25
    Crashes and Booms — 26
    Robots — 27
    Robot Apocalypse: May 6, 2010 — 28
    Relative Strength Index (RSI) — 29
    Flash, Short, & Long Term Trends — 31

Turning Points & Auction Behavior	32
PRACTICE - ANTICIPATE RESPONSES TO INFORMATION	33
PRACTICE - CRASH TEST	38
PRACTICE - BUY-AND-HOLD VS RSI	43
Critical question: why would there be a greater difference between RSI and buy-and-hold strategies over a shorter time period?	45
Critical question: is there such a thing as a hybrid strategy?	46

Chapter 4:
Basics of Investing — 47

Entry and Exit Strategy	48
Devaluation	48
Capital Investment	49
Distress	50
PRACTICE - INVESTING LEADERSHIP AND FOLLOWERSHIP	51
PRACTICE - IDENTIFY DIFFERENT LEADERS AND ATTEMPT TO EVALUATE THEIR USEFULNESS	53

Chapter 5: Basics of Market Externalities — 57

"OPTIMISM" is Reasonable	58
Depressions & the Great Depression	60
Cyclical Seasonality	62

Chapter 6: Introduction to Options — 66

Conclusion — 69

Appendix 1: History and Future of Markets	72
Appendix 2: Calculations	76

Correlation: for Understanding, Anticipation and
Prognostication of Economic Factors   76

Standard Deviation: Understanding What Factors Warrant
Correlative Analysis, Understanding Individual Companies
and Sectors in an Economy   83

Understanding how the stock market works is important, whether you have a retirement account with your employer, or want to invest for a living. Using basic skills like addition and subtraction, the principles of economics are learned through guided practice in common trading and investing methods, auction theory and tax implications of various investment strategies. Students learn to then apply these basic math skills to undertake sophisticated economic analysis and gain the ability to estimate current values of a stock and anticipate its future value too. Includes brief history of the Stock Market for conceptual context to understand the reasons why the market is the way it is today.

Chapter 1: Introduction to the Stock Markets

CHAPTER SUMMARY

Students will be generally introduced to the stock market, its history and functionality, and thereby understand the way it works, and its potential applications to their own lives

History of Stock and Exchanging Stock

Primitive forms of corporations that arose before the bronze age began, such as the partnership, remain in existence today, side by side with the most modern variants of the cooperative corporation, presenting a diverse economic ecosystem in which millions of businesses coexist in direct competition for the limited resources they all require.

To obtain the necessary resources for establishing or expanding operations, these corporations have at their disposal numerous means: but frequently, they will borrow what they lack, whether at interest or a SHARE of the returns or ownership in the equity of the corporation. When they share their returns with their investors, these investors develop both a legal and practical ownership interest in the affairs of the business they have invested into, and have in many cases demanded a say in how the corporation was run.

While sometimes this interest has been used for nefarious purposes, it is much more typical that the interest develops into a mutually beneficial partnership which benefits both investor and business equally.

Selling Stock Requires Monetization

When this ownership interest becomes transferrable by sale, the smallest unitary division of that ownership interest is referred to as "a share" of the stock. While sometimes fractions of shares are owned, the unit by which the entire stock is measured is in whole shares: just as we would talk about a distance measured in miles, even if we could divide those miles into fractional quarter miles or half miles.

When these shares are transferred by sale, they are valued in terms of money, currency. But they are not money. So, a stock may be sold for so many dollars, or euros, or yen, etc. Just as apples might be sold for so many units of currency. These monetary values themselves fluctuate, and for those of us who would own foreign stock valued in non-native currencies, the exchange rate of these currencies can affect the actual value of the stock we own: though a stock may remain worth ¥100, if the yen becomes worth more euros, though that stock may have been worth €0.86, it might now be worth a full €1. And so if we sell ¥100 of Japanese stocks to buy €1 in European stocks, we have effectively acquired the same amount of assets, but more euros.

Valuation of Money

Understanding that currency is not wealth, but the measure of it, is difficult: but a loaf of bread is a loaf of bread, whether it is sold for a dollar, or five, or five hundred yen.

Is that bread worth a dollar? Or five? Is five hundred yen worth five dollars? Or even the loaf of bread? What if the loaf of bread could be bought for five dollars and sold for more than five dollars in yen? We will learn the answers to these questions lie in the evaluation of what the stock entitles the owner to.

Sometimes stock entitles the owner to a share of the profits of the corporation: this dividend is paid out sometimes annually, sometimes more frequently, sometimes irregularly.

But all stock entitles the owner to a share of the total assets of the corporation, should it ever dissolve. It is in anticipation that the assets will increase, and that the profits will be distributed, that stock gains value. And when it is anticipated that assets will diminish, or that profits will not be distributed as they have been, that stocks lose value.

Consequently, when stock gains value, this means only that the owners of it hold it more dearly and will sell it only at a high enough price to justify their loss of ownership interest in the growing company. And when stock loses value, this means only the owners of it desire to sell it, to recover their money before it is devalued.

It does not mean that the company or its profits are worth more or less. And changes to the company's profits or wealth **do not impact stock price**. The stock price is affected by how much the owners of that stock wish to hold onto it, or sell it for different stock - or other things entirely, whether loaves of bread, medical treatments, a house, or even a new car.

When Stock Prices are Anticipatory: Bull and Bear Markets

Understand all stock prices are anticipatory, reflecting a future valuation: if an owner of stock values the future worth of the stock highly, or more highly than alternative uses for the money offered for that stock, they will be less likely to sell until a higher price is offered. If an owner of stock does not value that future worth of stock highly, they will be more inclined to sell.

Then understand this future valuation reflects the realized present value of all future time periods, ranging from a second in the future to decades or hundreds of years in the future when the assets that the stock represents an interest in are sold or are wasted. For this is the opportunity cost of selling the stock. All companies eventually go out of business. So the owner will want to sell before then - but assessing whether the company is worth as much as it ever will be, or whether there is some growth left, is a decision that affects the buyer's willingness to offer money for that stock.

Both demand and supply in this calculation are affected by future valuations.

This valuation is undertaken through an auction process in which those selling stock are able to bully the buyers into offering a higher price (which we call a bull market: the price of stock increases). And those buying stock are able to bear the pressure of those bullies to reduce the price demanded (which we call it a bear market: the price of stock decreases).

This is not the actual origin of the names of these markets: the bear and bull are animals whose lifecycle and behaviors are symbolic in nature, the colorful terms originate in 17th century poetry.

When Stock Prices are Reactionary

Some buyers and sellers do not care for the future, but are reactionary. They react especially to signs of distress: these vultures (to continue the animal imagery) and look for those companies which are nearly dead, or dying, hoping to feast on the carcass, selling off the assets in a competitive bidding process.

There are also other scavengers, who buy stock "on sale," bottom fishing, and looking to take advantage of irrational sellers.

And there are also predators, who like wolves will utilize their powers of control obtained by stock ownership to take down stock prices intentionally, to facilitate scavenging.

And there are still other buyers and sellers who do the opposite of these wolves, who, like cowherds, seek to feed or boost the assets of the company and either facilitate a bull market or "milk" the stock by benefiting from cheaply obtained dividends. These are typically ideological traders: they believe in the work undertaken by the company. Or because founded it.

When more stock is willing to be sold than be purchased, the increased supply of the stock drives its price lower; supply is also sometimes increased by the company when it sells additional shares of stock, either from its reserves (those shares it has retained to sell to raise money) or by establishing new shares to dilute the previously sold shares.

When more stock is willing to be purchased than sold, the diminished supply drives the price higher: demand exceeds supply, and competitive bidding takes place. This occurs when no new stock is issued or sold, and thus competitive bidding presents the normal state of a stock market.

The Stock Market

The marketplace in which stock is bought and sold is called the stock market. Just as you would go to a farmers market to buy or sell farm products, but also to engage in other activities, like enjoying some local music, the stock market has numerous other products that are traded. These lie outside the scope of this book and will not be presented in any great depth, but bear introduction here in the present context.

The first market for exchanging stock was held before history could record it with writing. However, the earliest written news reports on the activities of a stock market were made during the Republican era of ancient Rome: a common corporation at the time (a form of partnership similar to a "guild," where artisans would combine resources into a single company to bid for government work, purchasing their interest by share) had entered into a boom cycle. Cicero is recorded to have presented a report to the Senate in which he believed that the cost of these shares had grown too high. Today, you will hear similar opinions about any given stock being too high in price for what it is worth. And opinions that the price is too low, too. But not usually with the eloquence of Cicero: it is doubtful anyone will be recalling the business section of the Wall Street Journal thousands of years from now.

Opinions on the proper valuation of stock are as old as the market itself. It goes to show that the precise valuation of stock remains elusive to economists. And it likely always will be uncertain to some degree. This is because, even though our mathematical skills have improved far beyond the simple arithmetic of the paleolithic, the complex interaction between the realized present value of stock and its future value is dynamic, and fluid. And is still today beyond the ability of our mathematics to perfectly estimate. Even with our superior present mathematical and scientific knowledge we know now that the precise value of a stock cannot be known, except within a tolerance of error, because at this time it seems you cannot know both the present and future value of a stock at the same time, since one affects the other.

Therefore we may understand the value of stock within a degree of certainty, or with certainty within a range of prices, for either a particular time period in the past or future, but never for the present.

And it is fortunate that there is uncertainty. Because where there is uncertainty there is opportunity for profit.

This uncertainty is the source of profit in stock trading: if a stock might be undervalued, a trader will purchase the stock in the stock market, and sell it for a profit... or sell a stock which is overvalued at the market. The greater the uncertainty, the greater the opportunity for profit.

Uncertainty is fed by ignorance. Sometimes, ignorance is increased by misinformation, and outright lies. Therefore laws have been made (and broken) requiring the freedom of information, and the full disclosure of information. Accounting has been standardized by law, but there have been found ways to introduce unstandardized elements into this legal framework.

This is because it was understood that information affected profit: information itself is valuable, since so much depends on correct and available information. Now, information is itself traded - for a price.

Even the speed at which information is obtained can reduce your uncertainty faster than your competitor at the market, permitting you to profit from their ignorance.

Therefore, it is a sometimes relevant fact of our modern economy that the cost of information limits the rate at which a trader may successfully profit from their enterprise.

Communication also affects the ability to profit: if the command to buy or sell cannot be executed timely, the opportunity is lost.

When information is more or less accurate, and complete, the true value of a stock is known, and traders cease to be profitable: then, the stock market is useful only for investors. Prices tend to stabilize in environments of adequate information. Traders, who rely on uncertainty, and instability, sometimes will intentionally destabilize a market for profit. This is frequently a criminal action.

Manipulation is sometimes undertaken also by investors, who will create false demand or false supply of stock by buying or selling vast quantities, either at once, or over a long period of time, to pressure prices up or down. Pressuring the prices up, they can afford to sell the stock they bought at a profit, since they were able to amass quantities of stock before they pressured the price up. Pressuring prices down, they may afford to buy at a profit, anticipating the return of normal prices when they have stopped their manipulation. Manipulators are also criminals.

Sometimes, stock is purchased to gain a controlling interest in a company: when a stockholder owns a majority of stock, and that stock is vested with voting powers to administer the company, they may direct the company at will. These takeovers may be hostile or friendly, intended to eliminate a competitor, consolidate a competitor, or liquidate a competitor. Or, sometimes, to affect the stock price for predation or boosterism. That the very business model of a company can be changed when ownership changes opens up business to political intervention.

Global trade has always spread innovations, especially those of financial nature, quickly: trading partners need to be using similar corporate forms, similar currency, similar language, similar numbers. International trade today continues to shape the supply and demand for similar stock around the world corporations compete for the same pool of resources provided by investors and traders.

Membership in markets has always been limited, and brokers were necessary and expensive intermediaries. But in the 21st Century individual investors and traders successfully shifted this control from brokerages using the internet: by forming proxies of trading companies like Scott Trade (which became "TD Ameritrade" and is now "Charles Schwab"), individual investors could effectively trade stock with each other, and in the market, without a broker. Or brokerage fees. Incidentally, this innovation itself required stock issued to help fund its development and expansion.

This book is intended for this sort of individual investor so they may better understand the economic and business principles and models of both trading and investing in stock.

And who must rely on unreliable information.

Chapter 2: Introduction to Auctions

CHAPTER SUMMARY

Students will understand the principles of auction systems, including the bid / ask as it applies in forward, reverse and combination auctions. Students will understand buy and hold strategies that develop in the english auction system, dutch auction system, japanese auction system and the timed auction (candle auctions) as they arise in the stock markets. Students will understand the principles of trading strategies, including price bullying in asking a higher price ("bulls"), bearing pressure in bidding low ("bears"), identifying the strategies of other traders active in a market, and the role and advantage of valuation in predatory behavior.

Swapping and Trading

Barter is undertaken in many ways, sometimes a swop is performed, in which one thing or bundle of things is exchanged evenly for another without clear understanding of the value of either position, upon the assumption that they are of equivalent value. This evolved into a process of trading, in which things were exchanged sometimes for unequal value, in the knowledge that another barter would be undertaken to transform the loss into a gain: such as trading gold for cheap glass beads, and those glass beads for real estate worth far more than that gold was worth.

We will first discuss trading. Trading is a behavior in which an inventory of stock is purchased for resale: it is understood that the stock will not be held, and so exchanging money or other stock for a losing position is sometimes desired if it is known that the position will be sold again for a profit. So, in this sense, trading is essentially a retail practice. Traders will undertake numerous strategies to obtain stocks that they anticipate will appreciate in value due to either increasing demand, or shortening supply.

This trading strategy differs from investing, which is a behavior in which inventory of stock is purchased for ownership interest, either for their returns of profit in the form of dividends, or for their appreciating value of assets.

However, even investors must eventually exit the market, and when they do so, they must behave like traders: however, since their inventory represents stocks not in current retail circulation, their behavior models that which is similar to wholesalers: wholesaling investors are the source of inventory for retailing traders.

Whether purchased or sold for trading or investing, stocks are bought and sold in the stock market through an auction process: stocks do not have price tags.

Price Tags

The price tag was innovated in the early 20th Century as an expression of Quaker Christian philosophy, and introduced a new and standard means of commerce: buying and selling has become radically different in the modern age of the price tag, which presents an unnegotiable price offered to every potential buyer by the seller.

The Quakers believed it was immoral for different customers to pay different prices for the same item. In the 1870s, Macy's in New York (Rowland Hussey Macy was a Quaker) began affixing physical tags to items, eliminating haggling. This allowed shorter training time for new clerks (who would no longer need to know the art of haggling nor the range of accepted prices for every item) and allowed clerks to serve more customers. It also permitted self service retail and the development of the Super Market.

English or Forward Auction

However, older methods of bargaining are still utilized. Especially in the stock market. And foremost among these is the auction.

In the Stock Market, buyers and sellers each develop their own price based upon what they estimate a share of stock is worth. Necessarily, the lowest asked price among the sellers is going to be the first purchased by the highest bidded price among the buyers: the process is quite orderly, and self-organized - buyers necessarily want the cheapest price possible, and sellers naturally want the highest price possible. When there are no more buyers willing to offer such a high price, sellers must deal with those who would offer a lower price and the price at which stock is transferred falls; when there are no more sellers willing to offer such a low price, buyers must deal with those who would offer a higher price, and the price at which stock is transferred rises.

BID	BUYER	SELLER	OFFER
1st	$1	$10	1st
2nd	$2	$9	2nd
3rd	$3	$8	3rd
4th	$4	$7	4th
5th	$5	$6	5th
6th	$6	$5	6th
7th	$7	$4	7th
8th	$8	$3	8th
9th	$9	$2	9th
10th	$10	$1	10th

The bid price represents the maximum price that a buyer or buyers are willing to pay. The offer price represents the minimum price that a seller or sellers are willing to receive. In the above example, buyers who bid only $2 will find only two sellers who are willing to sell at that price (number 9 and 10, who will accept $2 or $1). If two buyers bid $2, only one will get $1, the other would have to pay the full $2. The buyer who bids $8 will find 8 sellers. The seller offering at $10 will only find one buyer at that price. If another seller wanted to get $10, the best they could do is $9, and would have to lower their price.

The word "auction" comes from the latin, augeo, "I increase," referencing the verbal call made as purchasers competed with each other to offer a higher price to the sellers in a "forward" auction. This "English" auction system of out bidding is typical of most auctions where the items being sold are atomistic, or easily interchangeable, divisible, undifferentiated and easily valued by a variety of sellers. It is also common in a seller's market in the stock market, where sellers competing with each other for a buyer will accept the bidding of the buyers.

In English Auctions only the seller's willingness matters: this is a bull market, with sellers encouraged to bully buyers to accept higher prices.

When prices are going up, you know this is the type of auction you're entering into.

Dutch or Reverse Auction

However, when items being sold are fairly unique by a limited number of sellers, or rare, or difficult to estimate, auctions are structured so that sellers compete with each other for buyers by reducing their price in a "reverse auction." Real estate is typically sold in this "Dutch" method where prices are asked, and then reduced until sold. This is common in a buyer's market in the stock market: buyers competing with each other to secure a seller will accept the prices asked by the sellers. This is also frequently observed when investors have controlled virtually all the stock of a company, and begin to sell of some to traders.

In Dutch Auctions, only the buyer's willingness matters: this is a bear market, with buyers bearing against the pressure of sellers, forcing them to lower prices.

When prices are going down, you know this is the type of auction you're entering into.

Japanese Auction

The "Japanese" auction is an advanced model, combining the English and Dutch methods by limiting the number of buyers and sellers by placing a price on entry, and forcing them to raise their bid (or lower their ask) at each round of bidding as the price of participation increases - upon penalty of being excluded from the auction if this price is not paid to the seller.

It is very similar to how in a round of poker everyone must meet the ante, or the last wager, to stay in the game. Eventually only a single buyer and/or seller is left, and they then directly engage with the buyers or sellers unimpeded by competition.

The Japanese method is seen only occasionally in the stock market, in situations where a buyer is trying to monopolize the stock, or when limited or new quantities of stock are available only from a monopoly, such as with an IPO. It is also seen whenever reserves of stock are sold by companies to investors.

However it is important to understand that when this is observed or occurs in a free stock market, this is not a true or structured form of Japanese auction: no one is requiring the ante be met, it is the natural result of market dynamics. But, like the English and Dutch methods, we use this theory to understand market behavior.

Timed Auction

A timed auction is one in which buying and selling can only be undertaken during a particular period of time (such as how long a candle burns, hence its also being known as the candlestick auction). In a free market, this occurs when a company has an artificial deadline for reporting financial information, or when a buyer or seller must pay tax or medical or other significant bills and cannot hold onto their position after a particular point. Every month, millions of buyers must purchase stock as part of their employer sponsored retirement plans, every year taxes come due and there is incentive to capture losing positions before the end of the calendar year, etc.

Free Market Behavior

The stock market functions as a combination of all these methods. Simultaneous forward and reverse auction systems can be observed with multiple buyers and multiple sellers competing in different ways for the same stock. Thus, one trader or investor may be undertaking strategies as if it were a Japanese auction, while another would behave as if it were a Dutch auction, and yet another might behave as if it were an English auction, while yet another trader is facing a deadline to make a trade and will behave like it were a Candlestick auction. These strategies often evolve out of the underlying behavior of the trader or investor: whether they are bears, bulls, vultures, wolves or boosters. Eventually, one or another behavior prevails into a trend.

It is important here to understand the strategies each trader or investor undertakes are dynamic, and fluid. Depending upon the kind of stock being competed for, or the nature of the market for that stock, or conditions of the market. So you will see elements of the Candlestick, Japanese, Dutch and English methods in almost every day of trading. When a buyer or seller develops more or less information about the value of a stock, or the quality of the stock becomes more or less atomistic, the character of its auction subtly changes. As the market for that individual stock becomes more or less bullish or bearish, or if general market conditions become more or less bearish or bullish, or if there are more or fewer investors scavenging distressed stocks, or more or fewer boosters, these strategies change dynamically and fluidly.

Therefore the individual trader or investor should be familiar with all these kinds of strategies and methods, able to identify the behaviors of their competitors and those buyers or sellers sitting across the table from them - so they can readily adapt. When wolves attack, and cannot be fended off by the boosters, it is advantageous to adopt the behavior of a vulture.

Critically, the decision of whether to wait for a higher or lower price, or to adjust your bid or ask, must depend on your estimation of not only the value of the stock you are trading or investing in, but also how everyone else values that stock also, and their behavior as they seek to obtain the same resources you want.

In this sense, even if a stock is fundamentally worthless, if it is highly demanded, it will deserve a higher price, since retailers will be easily able to sell their inventory; if a stock is fundamentally valuable, but undemanded, it will suffer among the penny stocks since retailers cannot sell their inventory.

The role and advantage of proper fundamental valuation in engaging with the behaviors and strategies of all those others in the market is that these empower a trader or investor to understand the role of demand on the stock's price.

The individual trader in this way functions through a retail business model: seeking to obtain stock which will become more valuable or demanded later, at a price that permits profit. Bargain hunting guides the inventory held. Because even the most dedicated investor will one day want to trade their stock, if they find a better deal.

This bargain hunting is best understood through the strategy of predation: because getting a good price when buying means the seller gets a bad price (the buyer preys upon the seller's ignorance) and similarly, getting a good price when selling means preying upon a buyer's ignorance. Sometimes by affecting their perception of the fundamental value of a stock, or its demand.

What the predatory wolf must not do is illegally modify the value of the stock by controlling information, or other criminal behaviors.

To keep with the animal imagery, we will describe this as hunting bears and bulls: rather than hunting the stock itself based on its fundamental values, the predatory wolf will instead make its prey the bears and bulls who would over or undervalue a stock based on overestimations of its present or future demand in trade.

Chapter 3: Basics of Predation

CHAPTER SUMMARY

Students will understand how to undertake predatory behaviors of bargain hunting, trend following, and be introduced to the advantages and disadvantages of robotic assistance. Students will understand how to both defend themselves against robots, and take advantage of robots, utilizing the limitations of their programming. Students will be introduced to illegal market manipulation, and understand how to defend themselves against bear and bull manipulators.

Crashes and Booms

Stock market crashes and booms are the results of traders mimicking the buying and selling behavior of each other, or of industry leaders, creating positive or negative feedback loops.

Booms and crashes occur not only after but in fact due to prolonged periods of stability in the market, either in equilibrium price, or in stable upward or downward trends.

This is because during periods of stability untrained, uneducated, inexperienced traders gain confidence to enter the market and mimic what industry leaders are doing. As the numbers and activity of these mimicking traders increases, information becomes confused: who is to easily tell who are experienced leaders or inexperienced followers? What should inexperienced followers imitate?

As inexperienced traders become unable to distinguish between what industry leadership is doing from their own inexperienced activity there results instability. And this in turn results in irrational selling or irrational buying. As this irrationality intensifies, it further destabilizes the market, creating false demand signals and false supply signals which can confuse even expert traders.

Eventually, the market booms or crashes depending on if there has been established a positive or negative feedback cycle: this cycle becomes stronger as all traders resonate in their decision making. In booms, confidence in the purchase of a stock at a higher price is justified by an ever increasing stock price; in crashes, confidence in purchasing erodes due to ever decreasing stock prices.

Eventually, corrections from booms inexperienced investors who sold their positions at a loss are wiped out, and cease their activity in the market leaving only experienced buyers. Then, the market restabilizes as only expert traders remain.

Robots

Recently, innovations in artificial intelligence have permitted mechanized trading. Programs have been designed by traders (whether novice or experienced) to act automatically, and also as "self-guided" or "self-advised" advisors (from which the term "Expert Advisor," or EA derives) - autonomous algorithms that either augment or guide the trader's behavior. We call these mechanized traders "robots," though in fact the term only correctly describes the autonomous mechanized traders: the mechanized traders who are advisors or guides are better understood through the colorful term, cyborgs, since they are merely embedded tools of human trading.

But we shall refer to all mechanized traders as "robots." For, whether or not the robot is participating with a human, the human tends to behave as mechanically as their mechanized guide or advisor.

It is important to understand how robots think. Current AI relies on a behavior of mimicry known as "machine learning." Even human-advised AI's undertake machine learning, and the true robots are programmed to be purely responsive by nature. They are not creative. They respond to predefined stimuli - both very fast, and very effectively.

Consequently, robots are increasingly the cause for crashes and booms, and generalized market instability. This destructive behavior is disadvantageous to their owners. However, they remain popular and increasingly used because there is a false belief that these machines can overcome the limitations of their programming: however, without creativity, they cannot.

And there is also the impression that quicker is better: sometimes their owners even believe they may profit from the booms, without paying the cost of the crash, if they can buy low and sell high before the crash. This thinking is just like amateur traders though. Through innovative algorithms and programs that can more quickly trade than their competitors: if their robots can buy and sell more quickly, and stop before anyone else notices the correction is coming, they can profit from the irrationality of slower robots.

Therefore, preying upon robots is no different than preying upon novice traders, and may in fact be easier, since these machines are necessarily more "emotionally" driven than an average human trader will be and less adaptive and resilient.

Another thing that these robots lack is imagination and foresight: the average human trader has the imagination to trust and hope, and foresight to understand that market conditions will improve after disturbance more than the profit of selling quick. Robots still do not yet understand this essential truth because they cannot experience what has not happened through imagination, and so are skittish.

Robot Apocalypse: May 6, 2010

The (financial) robot apocalypse began on May 6, 2010. It was that day that entire stock indices in the US fell 9% in a few minutes. Human traders quickly responded, and there was a recovery, but the terror was real. There was a real danger these machines demonstrated which could not be denied any longer.

Mechanical traders might indeed seem formidable at first: they can trade thousands of times faster than any human, from making calculations on the fundamental valuation of a stock, to calculating its relative demand, to executing buy or sell orders. However, human traders have in time learned these machines behave just like novice human traders. Albeit very fast ones.

To adapt and turn human slowness into an advantage traders learned to utilize the predictability and lack of foresight of the robots against them: their behavior may be anticipated well in advance by the trader who is willing to spend their time in thoughtful study. Now, robots largely battle one another over second to second trading, while humans take advantage of the ignorance of robots to dominate longer term trades.

When human traders understood these robots were simply more rapid versions of the inexperienced human traders who own them, flash crashes and booms became less frightening: they were not in fact a new phenomenon, just the same phenomenon undertaken at breathtaking speed. And so, human traders could easily trust them to be self-correcting, like any other slower form of boom or bust. Courage in the face of crashes, and conservativeness in the face of booms, seeing through the variability to understand the equilibrium price of a stock, these are the advantages of human traders. Slowness and patience are safeties against the unrelenting speed of robots.

Relative Strength Index (RSI)

The weapon of choice against ignorant or inexperienced traders, both human and robotic, is the mathematical calculation known as the RSI (relative strength index). It is intended to chart the current and historical strength or weakness of a stock or market based on the closing prices of a recent trading period.

The RSI is a kind of "momentum oscillator," measuring the velocity and magnitude of directional price movements. Momentum is both the magnitude and velocity at a particular rate of the rise or fall in price. In simpler terms, the RSI computes the ratio of higher closes to lower closes, which successfully accounts for the wrong consensus of the market in calculating the real value of a stock: stocks which have had more or stronger positive changes have a higher RSI than stocks which have had more or stronger negative changes.

The relative strength index was developed by J. Welles Wilder and published in a 1978 book, *New Concepts in Technical Trading Systems*, and also in *Commodities* magazine (now *Futures* magazine) in the June 1978 issue. It was in response to inexperienced human traders causing instability of markets - long before machine trading was even imagined.

In the subsequent decades since the machines came to the market, RSI was tested and compared with other strategies by Marek and Sediva in 2017. The testing was randomized in time and companies and showed that RSI can still produce good results in the short term; however, in longer time frames, RSI still does not out perform the simple time tested buy-and-hold strategy, it merely matches it.

Wilder posited in developing his RSI that when price moves up very rapidly, at some point it is considered overbought. Likewise, when price falls very rapidly, at some point it is considered oversold. In either case, Wilder deemed a reaction or reversal imminent.

Therefore, upon this premise, Wilder reasoned that the RSI could measure the stock's recent trading strength, and this equated to its value to traders. The slope of the RSI is directly proportional to the velocity of a change in the trend. The distance traveled by the RSI is proportional to the magnitude of the move.

Wilder believed that ceilings and floors are indicated when RSI goes above 70 or drops below 30, but these thresholds are arbitrary. Nevertheless, traditionally, RSI readings greater than the 70 level are considered to be in overbought territory, and RSI readings lower than the 30 level are considered to be in oversold territory. In between the 30 and 70 level is considered neutral, with the 50 level a sign of no trend.

Wilder further believed that divergence between RSI and price action is a very strong indication that a market turning point is imminent. Bearish divergence occurs when price makes a new high but the RSI makes a lower high, thus failing to confirm. Bullish divergence occurs when price makes a new low but RSI makes a higher low.

Flash, Short, & Long Term Trends

Calculating the index over a period of time (a day, week, month, year, decade, etc.) is irrelevant to the conclusion of the mathematics: if the index is above or below 50, it indicates strength or weakness of the stock, whether the gains have been greater or less than the losses in that time frame.

Whenever the index falls closer to 50, the stock may be understood to be fairly valued, this may help you understand the equilibrium price of a stock, at least under those present conditions.

As an example, we will look at oil. During an oil boom, the true value of an oil stock may rise; after the oil crash, the oil stock may actually have a much lower value. Understanding this helps highlight the need for the RSI to be applied to a correct time frame: before or after causational events. And this correlation still currently lies beyond the capacity for machines to understand: it lies beyond the ability of many humans to understand. It requires understanding the company itself, and what may affect its profitability and assets over a time frame spanning many booms and busts.

In a sense, the machines are retailers shifting inventory over minutes or days, and humans act as wholesalers to these machines over months and years - in the same way as investors act as wholesalers to human traders over years and decades.

Turning Points & Auction Behavior

Over the course of trading, consensus on the value of a stock results in periods of equilibrium for demand and supply, and the price that buyers and sellers settle on is described by boundaries called floors and ceilings: the floor is the price that sellers generally agree not to sell for less than, and the ceiling is the price that buyers generally agree not to buy for more than.

Sometimes these will shift, based on new information, in what is called an adjustment. If the information which resulted in that shift proves to be unreliable, the old floor and ceiling will generally be restored.

Some stocks will have a floor and ceiling which moves with the stock, as the stock gradually increases or decreases in value: however, this is rare. It may also simply be understood in terms of a rapidly adjusting floor and ceiling.

The ceilings and floors are easily interpreted through behavioral analysis. Examine the turning point.

When floors rise, this evidence shows that sellers are increasingly able to bully the buyers to accept higher prices, and by holding out for higher prices, encourage each other, and the market demonstrates augmentation auction behavior as the supply of stock for sale at lower prices is reduced.

When ceilings demonstrate a declining trend, this evidences buyers are increasingly able to bear the pressure of sellers to drive prices lower, and by encouraging each other to withstand the sellers, the market demonstrates a Dutch auction behavior as the supply of stock for sale at lower prices is increased.

These turning points, where auction behavior changes, where changes in the supply and demand for stock changes are the effect of information and trends in these ups and downs may be interpreted to understand the true value of the stock, adjusted for the effects of information through the RSI calculation.

PRACTICE - ANTICIPATE RESPONSES TO INFORMATION

Read the following news article. Then consider how different types of traders (bulls, bears, vultures, wolves and boosters) would react to it? What keywords would a robot pick up, and what reaction would ensue? What will investors think? Especially long term investors?

The strategy in a market determines whether this one news article results in a buy or a sale, and the lack of certain information raises the risk for potential profit or loss.

While we might react to this story in anticipation of how others would, if we disregard the potential reaction to this story as irrelevant, we notice that the company is paying a special dividend, and estimate based on past performance that it is unlikely that if bought after emotional reactions settle out the stock would crash beneath the extremely high dividend. Here, the assets are not essentially changing very much: even if the stock price is. It is reasonable to believe that the dividend would likely then return close to normal, but with a lower cost of stock to obtain that dividend, once the Brexit chaos calms.

Combining these two strategies, we would understand the Royal Bank of Scotland is a good buy, but it would be a better buy after emotional selling takes place. The minor loss to profitability during Brexit would not likely impact long term dividends very greatly. Therefore, it may make sense to wait a bit for the market to settle to a floor, and then buy up stock being oversold by skittish bears and robots.

Then, examine the price of RBS before, during and after this August news break, and you will see that the combined strategy, of picking a solid stock, then hunting bears and robots in that field, is being emulated by bulls and investors alike in the months following.

RBS hands £1bn dividend to taxpayers after unveiling bumper profits

Bailed out bank delivers special dividend but warns Brexit will cause it to miss performance targets this year

Ben Chapman @b_c_chapman
Friday 2 August 2019 09:07

Bailed out bank RBS delivered a rare £1bn windfall for taxpayers after announcing a special dividend on the back of surging profits, but warned uncertainty surrounding Brexit would cause it to miss profit targets this year.

The bank, which has been mired in a series of scandals going back more than a decade, will hand £1.7bn to shareholders including £1bn to the public purse by virtue of the Treasury's majority stake.

On Friday, RBS announced half-year profits attributable to shareholders were up 130 per cent on the same period last year to £2bn, its best performance for more than ten years. Operating profit was up 48 per cent to £2.7bn. Profits were boosted by further cost-cutting and the sale of Saudi bank Alawwal.

The improved results allowed RBS to pay a special dividend of 12p per share along with an annual dividend of 2p per share.

Despite higher profits, RBS shares fell 4 per cent in early trading off the back of a warning that 2020 performance targets may not be met. RBS said that a tough economic outlook would mean less demand for loans, causing it to miss profit and costs targets this year.

Outgoing RBS chief executive Ross McEwan siad: "Given the uncertain and competitive environment, we are focused on the areas we can control; costs are down, capital and liquidity are strong and we continue to grow lending to the real economy."

Donald Brown, senior investment manager at Brewin Dolphin, said RBS was now a very different bank to the one bailed out by taxpayers for £45.5bn in 2008 and was now "on the path to redemtion [sic]".

"While there are cautionary words around hitting some of it targets against the backdrop of Brexit, RBS appears to be in stronger shape," Mr Brown said.

"There are plenty of positives in these results, but its UK focus and the government's remaining stake will likely continue to weigh down the share price in the short term. The special dividend will provide a hard-earned £1bn boost to the Exchequer."

The fact that RBS is now profitable and finally beginning to pay money back to the public purse after ten years of losses totalling more than £130bn will again raise questions about the timing of the government's plan to sell off its shares.

Last year former chancellor Philip Hammond faced criticism for offloading almost 8 per cent of the bank's shares at a loss of around £2bn to taxpayers compared the bailout price.

RBS share price was 206p on Friday, less than half of the 502p per share the Treasury paid in 2008

SOURCE:
https://www.independent.co.uk/news/business/news/rbs-results-dividend-taxpayers-profits-rise-brexit-no-deal-a9035376.html

PRACTICE - CRASH TEST

Can you spot where there is a crash and a boom, and over the different time periods? Can you spot the floor and ceiling?

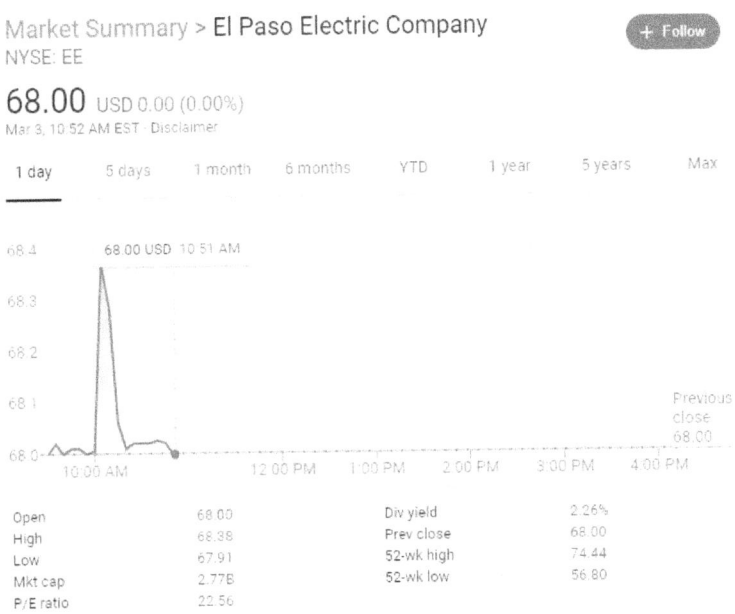

Here, the boom of nearly 40 cents per share occurred at 10am, and resolved in a few minutes, back to the exact price it was trading at before the boom, and also at the beginning of the day. The speed and precision of the boom is likely due to a positive feedback loop caused by primarily mechanized trading. The short duration and lack of correlating externalities indicates this is likely a wholly irrational boom. The floor here is $68, and the ceiling just under $68.40.

Here, we expand out our view to 5 days. Can you spot the crash? On February 27, at 9:30 am, over a few hours, the stock dropped suddenly about 80 cents. It then did not return precisely to where it had begun, but near to the anticipated decline if prognosticated over the course of a few days. This likely indicates a combination of mechanized and human trading. It coincides with the fourth quarter financial report by the company: the news initiated uncertainty about the value of the stock. After the adjustment, we see the floor established at $67.60 and the ceiling at just over $68.

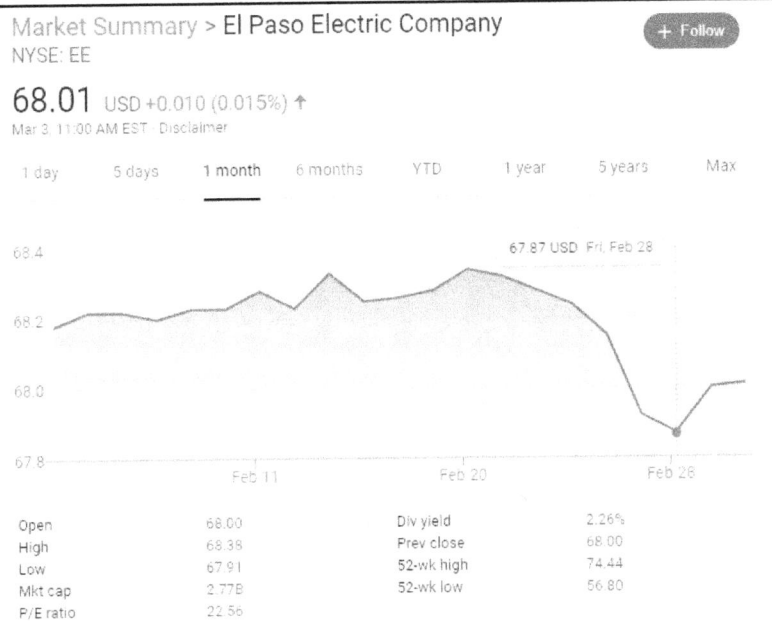

Let's expand to a month's time frame. Is this a crash, or an adjustment?

The answer lies on the next chart.

We can see this was an adjustment: notice the floor? The price hit the floor, and then rebounded. Here, the floor was just under $67.75 and the ceiling at $68.25.

Look at the time frame of a year, and you will see another adjustment, this one positive. On June 3, El Paso Electric agreed to be purchased in a friendly takeover by the Infrastructure Investments Fund, an Investment Vehicle Advised by J.P. Morgan Investment Management Inc. for $68.25 in cash per share: thus, the share value went up to about $68.25, and stabilized under the increased certainties of demand and supply. The initial drop after the first rise in price is due to some owners selling their stock after obtaining unusually high bids for it.

PRACTICE - BUY-AND-HOLD VS RSI

Compare and contrast the strategies of investing/wholesaling and trading/retailing by comparing and contrasting buy-and-hold versus RSI strategies

As an example, we will first look at Aflac, over a 20 year term.

20 Year Buy-And-Hold: Earns: $23.33, returning 192.17% or 9.60% per year

Buy at $12.14 on May 1st, 2000. Sell at $35.47 on April 1st, 2020.

20 Year RSI: Earns: $34.04, returning 193.44% or 9.67% per year

1. Short sell on October 1st, 2000 at $15.97. Buy on January 1st 2009 at $11.60.

Earns $4.37, returning 37.67% or 4.57% per year

2. Buy on January 1st 2009 at $11.60. Sell on August 1st, 2017 at $41.27.

Earns $29.67, returning 155.77%.

Granted, there was a crash at the end of this term, and we understand that the investor would not necessarily sell during a crash, and we also understand an trader would buy up that stock, but the value of the RSI in preventing damage from inexperienced traders is shown over the long term to be overrated: there is no substantial difference between the two strategies and the market cannot be timed over the long term.

Let's examine over a shorter time period. For this we will look at a different stock, Kroger, which presents the RSI strategy with both an open and close position - unlike most other stocks, Kroger stock rose during the crash of 2020.

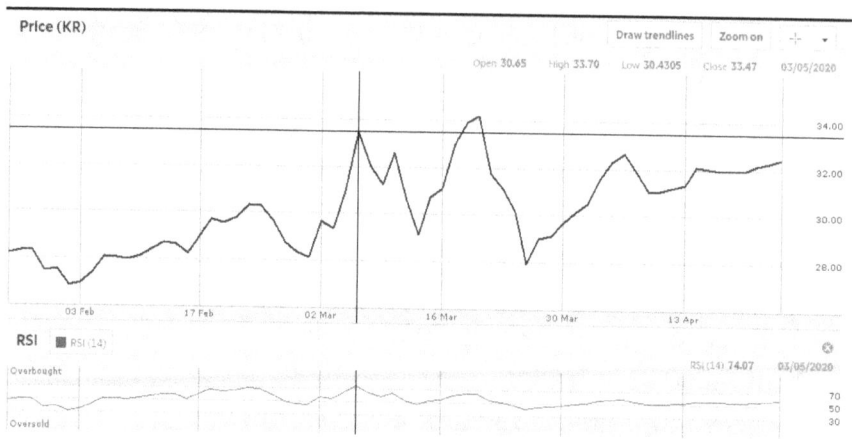

3 Month Buy-And-Hold: Earns: $3.98, returning 13.98% or 55.92% per year

Buy at $28.48 on January 24, 2020. Sell at $32.46 on April 23, 2020.

3 Month RSI: Earns: $6.07, returning 22.15% or 88.61% per year

Buy January 31, 2019 at $27.40. Sell on March 5, 2020 at $33.47.

Critical question: why would there be a greater difference between RSI and buy-and-hold strategies over a shorter time period?

Consider that over shorter time periods there is less information, and more variability.

Even in a well regulated market, there are simply fewer trades in a shorter time, and fewer opportunities for buyers and sellers to negotiate, through the auction process, the real value of the assets the stock represents. Experienced traders have fewer opportunities to hear the debate (as argued by sellers and buyers), and develop an informed opinion. Inexperienced traders have fewer opportunities to follow their leaders as they command the market with their bidding.

Also, the ability of one inexperienced trader (or predatory criminal) to affect the price of the stock over a short period is greater than over a long period: in the long term, eventually an inexperienced trader loses their money, and the criminal is arrested - or their victims discover the con - and the market stabilizes. There is no such opportunity for stability here.

Hence, over a shorter time, for retailing traders, RSI is the better strategy. And over a longer time, for wholesaling investors, buy-and-hold is a viable alternative.

Critical question: is there such a thing as a hybrid strategy?

There has been postulated that a hybrid strategy may be appropriate, combining buy-and-hold over a long term with the investor closing their position using RSI: when the stock is overbought, to sell. What are the risks and benefits of this hybrid strategy?

Answer: Because there is no real difference between RSI and long term buy and hold, there are no relative risks or benefits of this strategy, as they will result in the same outcome.

Chapter 4: Basics of Investing

CHAPTER SUMMARY

Students will understand investing strategies: the value of ownership interest in the form of profit (dividends) and appreciating assets, and the strategies of hostile and friendly takeovers, spinoffs, and distressed investment. And the exit strategy for investors: trading.

Entry and Exit Strategy

A different strategy from trading is investing: here, the buyers and sellers in the market are obtaining or divesting themselves of ownership interest, either for a return of the profit in that company by way of dividends, or in the form of a share in the assets which may be appreciating or depreciating.

Because all investors eventually exit their positions, and when they do so, they behave like traders, it is easy to conflate the two strategies: however, investors are not simply long-term traders.

Investors seek to buy stock in companies which will use the stock to fund capital expenses: capital expenses are those purchases which result in assets. By such capitalism, these companies both increase the amount of assets each shareholder owns, and also their profit.

Devaluation

Sometimes, the sale of stock will devalue each share: as the limited assets of a company are divided up into smaller and smaller parts, until the capital expenses are realized into assets, the cost per share will necessarily fall. However, this is sometimes compensated by a consistent or rising dividend, or share in the profits.

Consider, if a company's stock falls during its fundraising for capital expenses, but its dividend remains constant, the dividend payment per cost of share will increase. So, if for example, the cost per share falls 5%, but the dividend rate increases to 10%, each investor will recover the 5% in lost assets with 10% returned in the form of profits, to gain 5%. If they used those profits to simply buy more stock, they would end up with 5% more assets (in the form of stock) than they had started with.

Capital Investment

The investor is not necessarily a long term trader: some investments are short term. If a company is developing its capacity to earn more profit by increasing its debt, or undertaking other expenses, an investor will weigh the future profitability against the current value of the assets they are buying. For example, a power company investing in more efficient generators may require debt, and be expected to have less assets - until the new generators come on line, and the profits increase, to pay down the debt, and then accumulate more assets than the company had begun with.

An investor will look at the return to their investment in such terms.

Sometimes, investors may represent competitive interests: by buying ownership in a rival, they may either eliminate competition or bring that rival into a more efficient relationship of a cartel, conglomerate, or even a merger. In this situation, ownership power is itself an asset. The value of owning one's competitors motivates hostile or friendly takeovers: a friendly takeover is one which is sought by both rivals, whereas a hostile takeover is sought only by one rival. Some takeovers are neither hostile nor friendly, but represent a partially friendly or partially hostile takeover.

If it becomes known that a rival will be trying to buy up a majority share of stock, prices of the stock can be driven up, as the demand is anticipated to increase and supply shorten. But it may also have an adverse effect on the company undertaking the takeover, as this represents a greater supply of stock and reduced demand. Prices of stock in the company undertaking the takeover can also diminish if the shareholders do not believe that the purchase is resulting in an equivalent amount of assets. Especially if the takeover is being facilitated by an exchange of one company's stock for the other.

Occasionally, a company will "spin off" one of its enterprises, or a conglomerate will spin off one of its companies. The subsidiary will be sold off, to form a new company, frequently through issuing stock or by an exchange of stock. These kinds of activities represent an opposite to the takeover, with opposite effects on stock prices: the parent company may see a bump in its stock price, if shareholders believe the sale is resulting in an increase of assets - or efficiency, and as the equity represented by stock shortens in supply, and demand increases.

Distress

Sometimes, a distressed company will be invested in, understanding that it will be going bankrupt, or is currently undergoing bankruptcy. Distressed investing has two aims: liquidation of assets (hopefully at a profit to what they were purchased for in buying stock), and reformation through bankruptcy into a more efficient and profitable company. These two goals are sometimes undertaken simultaneously, as assets are sold off to both fund reforms through capital expenses and also improve efficiency.

The exit strategy for any investor is trading. Those owning stock will eventually seek to sell their interests. However, because an investor is not considering as a primary motivation the eventual value of their stock to potential buyers, they will make different purchasing - and holding - decisions than traders will. Investors do not chase shortening supply and increasing demand, they do not respond to changing stock prices in their holding decisions.

PRACTICE - INVESTING LEADERSHIP AND FOLLOWERSHIP

Investors, like traders, will look to leaders to help guide their decisions: this is why boosterism will also try to encourage purchasing behavior in investors. And why wolves will also encourage investors to divest their holdings.

There are many kinds of leadership both traders and investors look to, but to avoid boosters and wolves: an investment or divestment decision should be made without the influence of these ulterior motivations.

There are several major kinds of leaders.

The investment banker, mutual fund or holding company leadership. The inexperienced investor or trader will sometimes look to the leadership of investment banks, mutual funds, or holding companies - who are presumed to be experts in their own right, but also academically advised, and emulate their investment and divestment decisions. This is problematic, as sometimes the ability of an investor to understand what investment and divestment decisions are being made cannot be timely, or complete. With imperfect information, the inexperienced investor or trader will make imperfect emulation.

The academic leadership. The inexperienced investor or trader will attempt to compensate for their lack of formal education and training by utilizing the advice of academic leadership: economists, especially. Academic journals are sometimes used to curate the information, but more frequently, the inexperienced investor will rely on journalists, especially newspaper publishers, television producers and radio broadcasters to curate academic advice, and also present the academic advice in lay terms. This results in more or less imperfect information: and, unless the academic advice is specifically tailored to the investor or trader, the information will be imperfectly applied.

The expert leadership. Inexperienced traders will also look to experts in the field: successful investors and traders, whether practiced generally, or in a specific stock. Sometimes it is presumed that if the leadership of a company undertakes a dramatic shift in their positioning, either buying up a lot of stock, or selling a lot of stock, they know something that the common investor or trader doesn't know yet; sometimes, if a wealthy investor or trader suddenly undertakes a dramatic shift in their positioning, if there is a lot of stock bought or sold, it is presumed this indicates knowledge of something that is not known yet generally. However, it is frequently difficult to verify the veracity of these presumptions, even the presumption of whether a trader or investor is successful - and this can lead to all kinds of problems later on.

PRACTICE - IDENTIFY DIFFERENT LEADERS AND ATTEMPT TO EVALUATE THEIR USEFULNESS

Example: Berkshire Hathaway as a holding company, Yahoo! News as an academic advisor, and Warren Buffet as an expert.

The subtle tone shift from Warren Buffett every investor must note: Morning Brief
by Myles Udland, Markets Reporter: Yahoo Finance May 4, 2020

Warren Buffett sounds cautious.

At the Berkshire Hathaway (BRK-A, BRK-B) annual shareholders meeting on Saturday, Buffett began the proceedings by offering a roughly 75-minute overview of why American history offers reasons for investor optimism.

This is a familiar theme for Buffett. In the last several years he has written and spoken extensively about the "American tailwind" that investors can ride by investing in the stock market. And while Buffett reiterated this long-term optimism on Saturday, there was a subtle change in his message.

And investors should take note.

"I don't know, and perhaps with a bias, I don't believe anybody knows what the market is going to do tomorrow, next week, next month, next year," Buffett said Saturday. "You can bet on America but you have to be careful about how you bet. Simply because markets can do anything... Nobody knows what's going to happen tomorrow."

On the surface, these comments appear benign. "Warren Buffett says investors should think long-term" isn't much of a headline.

But Buffett's outline isn't that investors should think long-term right now, but that they must think long-term. In other words, there aren't many reasons Buffett can find to see the current situation as anything but challenging. And considering Buffett's long held bullish views, this is as bearish a take as we're liable to ever hear from Buffett.

And Buffett's recent actions speak louder than any of the words uttered during Saturday's meeting.

The biggest headline was Buffett's confirmation that Berkshire sold its entire stake in the country's four largest airlines — American (AAL), United (UAL), Delta (DAL) and Southwest (LUV). As Buffett outlined on Saturday, in his view the bet was simple: pay about $8 billion for these holdings to get back about $1 billion earnings.

The coronavirus pandemic and associated global economic shutdown changed this picture considerably. Buffett went so far as to tell the airlines: "I wish them luck."

Berkshire was also restrained in repurchasing its own stock during the quarter, spending just $1.6 billion buying back its own shares and conducting no repurchases after Mach 10. Morningstar analyst Greg Warren said he was "extremely disappointed" with this decision.

"While we can certainly understand the need to be cautious with investments and acquisitions in the near term...the company has a good investment opportunity in its own common stock and management should really be called out for failing to take more aggressive action during the first quarter," Warren added.

In response to a question about this decision on Saturday, Buffett said, "I don't think Berkshire shares are, at present value, at a significantly different discount than they were when we were paying somewhat higher prices."

Buffett added that, "We always think about [repurchasing stock], but I don't feel that it's far more compelling to buy Berkshire shares now than I would've felt three months, or six months ago, or nine months ago. It's always a possibility. And we'll see what happens."

And with that, Buffett more than says it all about his current view of Berkshire's stock and the market more broadly.

Berkshire shares were down 19% this year through Friday's close. Over the last year, the stock is down 15%. At any time in the last three, or six, or nine months Buffett would've been paying a significantly higher per-share price to repurchase stock.

And yet even with the market's current discount he doesn't think the stock is undervalued. And suggests he doesn't think much else is, either.

Critical questions:
- Do you trust Berkshire Hathaway as a leader? Would you emulate their decisions?
- Do you trust Yahoo! News as a leader? Would you let them advise you? To accurately present and summarize what Berkshire and Buffet are doing and saying?
- Do you trust Warren Buffet as a leader? Would you emulate his decisions?
- Examine American Airlines, United Airlines, Delta Airlines and Southwest Airlines for yourself: do you come to the same conclusion that these leaders do? Would their

advice and leadership impact how much you have confidence in your own decisions?
- What training, experience and technical skill do you lack to academically advise yourself? To become a leader?
- If you were to obtain economics textbooks from the library or internet, could you self-instruct? Could you obtain training from a local college or university? Hire a tutor, whether an undergraduate, graduate or Professor of economics?
- Even if you are a leader, what is the value of consulting with other leaders, through academic forums and debating the validity of each others' conclusions?
- In observing the debates and consultation of experts, what do you learn about your own role in the process of collaboratively discovering information?

Chapter 5: Basics of Market Externalities

CHAPTER SUMMARY

Students will learn the basics of market economics: the cyclical nature of seasonal behaviors ("summer vacation"), the capital cycle as it relates to agricultural and construction seasons. Students will understand the impact of political warfare, civil unrest, economic warfare and martial warfare on stocks. Students will understand the impact of inflation and the value of money on real stock value.

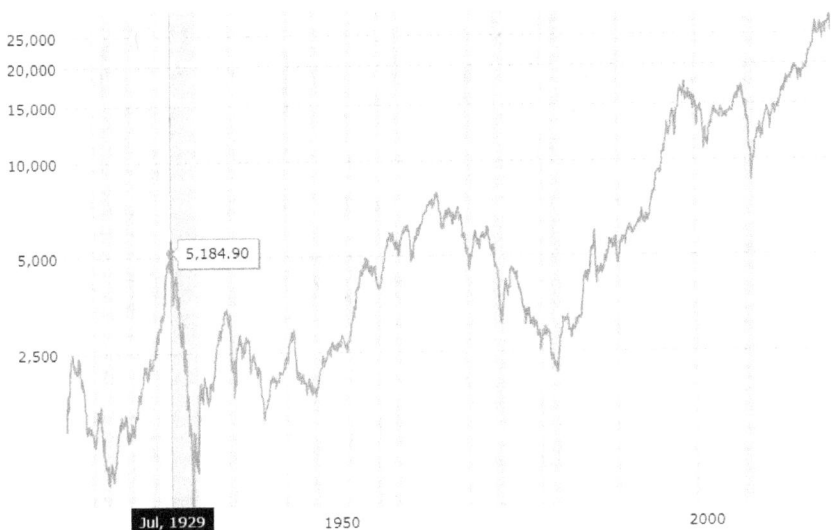

Looking at this 100 year chart of the Dow Jones Industrial Index, two facts should be apparent.

1. The market frequently gains during a recession, and
2. The market generally increases in value.

We will soon understand why these occur. For now, it is important you understand the fundamental lesson of this chapter:

"OPTIMISM" is Reasonable

It is a generalized fact that our losses are always temporary. This is not senseless optimism, nor overconfidence.
   This is the necessary conclusion of hundreds of years, thousands of years, of trading and investing.

And the reason has been mathematically understood and proven.

PROFIT = INCOME - EXPENSES. When EXPENSES are inevitably used for purchasing ASSETS, this functions as a kind of negative expense, for it increases our profit: therefore, the accumulation of ASSETS is justified; these ASSETS, minus their LIABILITIES = CAPITAL. Capital, a measure of wealth, naturally increases when incentivized by profit.

Therefore, the trader and investor should be bold. There is far more to be lost by not venturing than by entering the market, even untimely: if you think your skill unequal to the present demands upon it, remember that it is not by virtue of our skill that we stand to gain by our audacity, it is because of the fundamental nature of the economies we function within. With time, the skill and art of industry improves, technology advances, and the wealth of the companies whose stock we own increases: this wealth tends to drive an increased demand for our stock.

It is equally reasonable to conclude that what losses we do experience are largely not of our own making, but due to market externalities. Our losses are aberrations, and if we are able to simply weather them, and trust to the skill of our industry to adapt to whatever caused these set backs, we will emerge stronger than before.

Of course, one or two of our stocks may utterly fail us, but by diversifying our capital through indexing, we may trust to the law of averages: most companies will adapt, to thrive in the new economic conditions.

This confidence most new traders and investors struggle with: though the facts are clear, they remain pessimistic. They lack the direct experience to place their own losses in perspective. And, overwhelmed by fear, and doubt, sell untimely and indiscriminately. This is why it is important to study market histories carefully.

Depressions & the Great Depression

Yet after studying history should you yourself still feel this fear, or doubt, only stop to consider carefully that trading and investing is also an industry, and there is art and skill you may rely upon to improve as you adapt to new market conditions. You will thrive, given enough time.

The trader and investor alike face two primary externalities: inflation, and deflation. It is these that we will study the history of next, to better prepare you to adapt to the challenges you will face.

During the last 100 years, the Dow Jones crossed the $5000 level 9 times. The first time, it may have seemed very significant to some inexperienced traders like yourself. And the second time, when it crashed in the same year, it may have also seemed significant. At least to many traders who were unaware of this basic fact.

True enough, during that panic, the market dropped to its lowest point. But had an investor held on during that panic, they would have completely recovered their $5000 value within 25 years. But when accounting for dividends, this recovery takes only 10 years (dividends averaged a staggering 14% during the depression). And when accounting for the deflating value of money during that period, the real purchasing value of the dollars relative to the cost of the stock they purchase, the recovery time is actually less than 4.5 years.

The Great Depression was a deflationary period. And because the Consumer Price Index in late 1936 was more than 18 percent lower than it was in the fall of 1929, stating market returns without accounting for deflation exaggerates the decline.

Understanding the way that externalities affect the value of stocks, and the stock market itself, is very important to estimating the value of a stock.

If you could buy a ton of iron today, knowing that that iron would be more demanded in the future, would you pay more or less for that iron than it is presently worth? How much more or less? You would have to make sure that the amount you can sell the iron for in the future compensates you for the cost of not investing in other items or things which could potentially be worth even more in the same time period.

For example, if you could lend money for 5 years at 5% or 7%, you would choose the 7%.

It is important here to recognize that inflation, or deflation, can affect the return: if inflation occurs at 2% per year, the real return on either loan would be 3% or 5%.

And if iron were to be subjected to a different inflation index than say, for example, gold, this would affect the relative rates of return: choosing the material with the lower inflation rate would increase your wealth.

Also consider the costs of storage: it costs much less to store metals than it does to store orange juice. And some things cannot be stored: green bananas do not remain so for very long. No matter how well they are warehoused.

As bananas are not for investment, so too is gold not for trading. Therefore, there is an inclination to hoard for wholesaling gold, and the currency it represents.

This places at play the supply of currency, of wealth, which we measure in buying power. For there are times when the inflation rate naturally rises, and naturally falls, enticing the investor of currency to spend their money to buy material items that have more favorable valuation during the inflationary or deflationary cycle.

The investor who forgets they must one day return to trading, who no longer feels the desire and greed to increase their wealth, who fears venturing their capital, will slowly but surely lose their spending power to inflation. And the trader who forgets the seasonal cycles of money risks making bad trades.

Cyclical Seasonality

Even within a single fiscal year, there are four distinct seasons of money: these have traditionally been affected by agricultural cycles of planting and harvesting, of breeding and culling, and other natural agricultural cycles. And also to some degree the natural cycles of winter and summer which can impact shipping and other transportation and mining.

Some of these cycles are more pronounced in regional economies: a local power company will have more sales in summer and winter than in fall or spring because people wish to heat and cool their homes against the inclement weather. But a large interstate or international power company might not notice this seasonality.

Consider, how would this predictable seasonal change in revenue affect stock price? Would you see regular increases and decreases? Would you want to time your buying and selling accordingly?

On the following page, look carefully at the price of Xcel Energy Stock (XEL): as weather changes, the stock price regularly cycles.

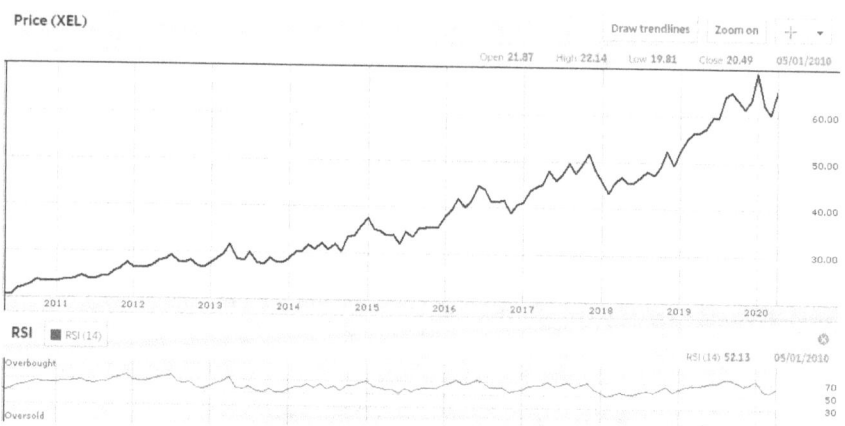

But beyond the weather, also at play is the just as natural cycle of vacations and recreation that leading partners of trading firms and banks participate in: no one wants to take a vacation when the weather is bad.

Over hundreds of years, these vacations have become institutionalized and customary to be scheduled in the summer, and it may be anticipated junior bankers and traders who are left in charge may be expected to be much more conservative and risk averse: no one wants to welcome the boss back to a loss due to some sketchy trading!

The banks and traders may also have access to more money after the harvest is in, after the minerals are extracted, after their clients have repaid loans. And senior traders always try to make their books look better at the ends of quarters, and the end at the of the year. Anticipating that senior traders returning from vacation with money to invest, and books to polish up, lets you predict they will rebalance their portfolios and should give you insight to when you should yourself participate (or avoid) the times when these expert traders and investors are more active.

And then there are also oligarchs manipulating markets, whether legally through hostile and friendly takeovers, or illegally through a variety of means of affecting the supply or demand for stocks, money, and even raw materials or hardball and hide the ball tactics. Or good old fashioned monopolization, intimidation, exclusion and hard business. These artificially inflate or deflate the buying value of a stock.

Today, the most influential externality is the news media. When robots, or others, get wind of news, their confidence increases and they will execute sales and buys that perhaps they might not have otherwise: whether the information is accurate or inaccurate, significant or insignificant, must be determined by careful investigation and collaboration. However, even inaccurate, insificant news can result in crashes or booms, which you can ride, or avoid: if it becomes rumored that there will be a friendly takeover, or that a crop has failed, or that there has been less demand for a product, these rumors can profoundly affect market prices.

A good retailer always keeps in stock those items which they anticipate will be demanded: the same rule applies in trading. Stock up in inventory on those stocks which you anticipate will be demanded due to news, and their value will increase: sell them to those shopping to cash in and you will make a profit.

A retailer also anticipates seasonal changes, switching out winter styles for spring ones, summer for spring, fall for summer. Keeping up on seasonal shifts in demand and supply is also an avenue for profit.

But it may also be a wiser strategy, if you are unable to anticipate these shifts, to choose to invest and trade in those stocks which are unaffected or less affected by externalities. It is very rare for a utility company to be affected by externalities, for example: the lights are always kept on, and the power company is so well insured even a major disaster won't disrupt profits much.

Chapter 6: Introduction to Options

CHAPTER SUMMARY

Students will understand what options are, and a basic trading strategy to capitalize upon consistent variability

"Options" is the term used to describe "options to buy" or "options to sell," and represent a contract by which the owner of the option agrees to sell or buy at a prearranged price at a prearranged date and time. If the option is not exercised at that date and time, it expires, and is valueless. The cost of these contracts are determined through an auction process identical to the stock market.

Options to buy and sell can be made on anything from stock, to commodities, to currency, etc.

However, due to the potential expiration, there arises a new dynamic to the trading.

If someone owns an option to buy at $10, but the actual value of the thing to be bought on the market is $9, the option is essentially worthless: why would you buy at $10 when you can buy on the market for $9? Similarly, if the option to sell is less than the market price upon expiration, the option is worthless.

Consequently, as the market value fluctuates, there are effects on the options market which are difficult to predict, and rapid swings in prices are not uncommon, especially as the contract approaches expiration.

Some contracts are sold and bought 5 minutes before expiration, others, 20 minutes, some hours, some days, some weeks, some months, sometimes they are traded a year or years in advance. Price volatility increases the closer to expiration.

Analysis of the underlying market value of the option provides insight into whether it is over or undervalued.

However, another strategy is to measure the volatility of the market and to use this total volatility as a guide for how to open and close a position.

For example, if the volatility is +/- $2 from $10, trading consistently between $8 and $12, it would be reasonable to open a position anywhere in that range, and close it for a profit before it exits that range: there is likely to be a buyer or seller who is willing to take the option prior to expiration. Consequently, the underlying market value is irrelevant.

A trader who earns a few cents or dollars on these trades does not earn much profit. However, by successfully trading dozens of times per hour, and buying or selling multiple options at every trade, the volume of these transactions can add up considerably.

Yet there is still the risk that the volatility can unexpectedly shift, or that the underlying market value could force an unforeseen adjustment: this strategy entails considerable risk. However, it allows the trader to limit their risk by keeping the profit margin lower than the anticipated volatility.

Option trading is both an art and science, and requires considerable practice: until you can successfully position and close with regular success, or at least more success than your failures incur losses for, it is unwise to enter the market.

Conclusion

In conclusion, I hope to have conveyed to you at very least the importance of valuing things with the resources and opportunities they may provide. A dollar could buy a loaf of bread, or an organic apple, or a share of stock in a microprocessor company, or even the rental of a motion picture. What we spend our money on is as important as how much money we have to spend, and when we invest, we should carefully consider our purpose.

And this has profound implications. For while the increase of wealth is a worthwhile goal, unless you are able to obtain satisfaction and happiness from those activities that allow your increased wealth, it is an expensive, unnecessary and ultimately unsatisfactory undertaking.

At the beginning of this course we discussed how stock is used by businesses to develop their capacity to undertake their industry. At the end, we discussed how these businesses rely on investment and trading of their stock to adapt to changing conditions within their markets, and other market externalities. The power of an investor or trader to choose to deal with companies which most benefit them requires fully assessing the ethical and moral behaviors of these companies: a company which improves the quality of life for its stockholders and stakeholders will better weather changing conditions and survive to profit longer than companies which sometimes literally undermine those people and institutions which would have supported them.

In my course on non-profit business, and capitalism, this concept is more fully discussed: and I would encourage any trader or investor to develop a better understanding of business if they would truly succeed in either trading or investing. Because the stock the trader and investor owns represents the assets owned by a business entity; the trader and investor are in very real terms owners of these businesses. And those businesses benefit when their stockholders are able to make informed decisions and remain active in both boosting and administering those companies. Quite as much as a trader or investor benefits by understanding why and how a company is profitable, and whether they are adaptable, and will sustain that profit in the long term.

And it is important to maintain a long-term perspective, even for a trader. For whether a position is held a few hours, or days, or even months, the trader must again and again enter the market during the course of their lives.

Just as every investor must return to the trading floor eventually, every trader must eventually reconcile their positions to understand they may have benefited as much or more to have weathered the downturn - no matter what the RSI told otherwise. Or they may find they are rebuying stock they just sold, because fundamentally that stock is worth holding over a long time.

At last, I would encourage your confidence. Be bold, be audacious! Courage - and its requisite optimism - is the defining characteristic of anyone who earns a living in the stock market. With adequate prudence, your bravery will pay dividends, and help those businesses you now own make this world a better place.

Should you invest in one stock or another should become a question of whether you should go into one line of industry or business or another. Hair salons, or hotels? Electricity or molybdenum? Consider carefully the needs of the world, and their demands, and then look for those businesses which are improving the quality of life for society by meeting those demands and needs. And which demonstrate the requisite skill to do so profitably. What company will best utilize your capital to grow through service and production, to do the most good?

Remembering your role in the development of society, take pride in your important work as a stock trader. By judging the best companies for the work at hand, you expedite the advancement of civilization. There is honor, and profit, in confronting the problems of the world, in giving companies hard at work the necessary capital to do that work.

So, try to forgive your early failures - and you will have many of them. For if you do, and learn from them, and try again, you will find the market will also be forgiving. In the market, there is no stigma, there is no prejudice: everyone can always have a fresh start, and a fair opportunity to earn a profit.

Finally, to that end, I would offer this advice: start small, but do start. You don't need to start with much, and as much as you may regret not having more to invest, the greater regret will be found if you never begin. You will find that as your confidence and experience grows, you will be able to venture more, that your strength will always match your opportunities. And this is a truly encouraging thought! For it implies that you will inevitably find that prosperity you seek.

Aaron Scott Brachfeld

Appendix 1: History and Future of Markets

Corporations have existed since the stone age, and ownership in them was as easily traded and exchanged as they are today. When the innovations of the labor union subsequent cooperative corporations in the Bronze Age of Egypt were combined with those advances of globalized accountancy at in contemporary Southeast Asia, a financial revolution was first able to be contemplated: the rise of modern banking and financial institutions required the capacity of governments to establish, manage and regulate not only its own debts, but those of corporate ownership. By the time Rome had arisen as a regional power, the Senate there had discovered the means by which both corporations and governments might manage supplies of commodities and even the value of money - and imposed upon its dominion the necessary laws to prevent unhealthy and dangerous exercises of power.

Yet it was not until the 12th Century in France that brokerages were utilized to facilitate an increasingly complex financial system: banks began to hire "courtiers de change" to act on their behalf; these courtiers also acted on behalf of agricultural communities. It was not long, perhaps less than a generation or two, before these brokers gained their independence: the first independent brokers of recorded history were in Bruges; they met at a local inn owned by the Van der Beurze family, and so as a gesture of humor, called themselves the Brugse Beurse - but began to increasingly organize themselves into an institution distinct from both banks and dealers, complete with regulations upon which membership relied.

The brokerage revolution quickly spread, first in and around Flanders, then to nearby countries: international traders brought the idea back to their home countries, where they understood the economic potential of this peculiar institution and established their own "Beurzen." The Italians advanced the idea further, and their "Borsa" grew beyond inns to specialized buildings for trading debt and ownership instruments, and these were standardized to facilitate trade. This technological innovation was adopted into the German Borse, the Russian Birza, the Czech Burza, the Swedish Bors, the Norwegian Bors, etc. It is merely coincidental (but convenient) that the name of the original innkeeper was akin to the Latin "Bursa," or purse, or money bag: for this is what these independent brokers represented, the pursers of the bank and the pursers of the dealers.

Less than a hundred and fifty years after the first proto-market was held at an inn in Flanders, by 1350, brokers discovered how to weaponize their power and manipulate the value of commodities, currencies and debts, and then dealing in government securities, sought to destabilize these governments. This led to laws passed in 1351 by the Venetians, Pisans, Veronans, Genoans, and Florentines. Some of which were effective.

By the 16th Century, companies began to issue what would be recognizable as modern type share certificates, and this permitted the innovation of fixed capital stock by 1602 permitted continuous trade in stock certificates: the Dutch East India Company utilized this innovation to develop secondary markets in options and repos, which permitted short selling (until it was briefly banned in 1610 - it is even today still highly regulated because it is dangerous).

With the advent of Communist theory, stock markets were illegalized in Communist nations, being understood by their economists as essential to Capitalism. Though their understanding was flawed, and capitalist systems evolved in the communist nations despite this precaution, and many modern communist countries do have a stock market, it did permit a glimpse through the re-evolution of stock markets (in terms of quasi-markets, underground/illegal markets, and the re-emergent markets after the fall of communism) of the vital elements of stock trading - the same process by which modern markets evolved were repeated, indicating that there were fundamental and sequential requisites of technology and understanding to the development of stock markets.

This lends credence to the supposition that the process of evolution and development is as yet incomplete, and that future innovations will permit an even more sophisticated means of financing debts, likely after the development of some new secondary market or corporate or legal innovation for assigning ownership.

Already, new corporate entities have been seen to evolve in the freest markets: in Colorado during the last 50 years we have already seen the innovation of a non-profit bank owned by a for profit corporation, non-profit cooperative banks, and even secondary markets for commodity certification. To a T, every and all of these Coloradoan innovations have been aimed at circumventing federal regulations, frequently those pertaining to commodity trading. Therefore, it may be reasonable to speculate that the future of stock markets will involve an innovation of some kind of money brokerage: if not by the development of an actually effective quasicurrencies, protocurrencies or cryptocurrencies, then by the development of quasimunicipal corporations.

Excitingly, even in Grand Junction efforts to obtain this goal have already been attempted as Clifton periodically seeks its independence from Mesa County for the establishment of free enterprise zones. But in Denver deregulation is already occurring; Walsenburg largely deregulated its real estate, emulating an already liberal Delta County. However, the answer need not come from Colorado at all: however, the unique conditions here, combined with the encouraging attitude of the Democratic controlled legislature and executive toward free markets, suggests that it is as likely to occur somewhere in the Rocky Mountains as anywhere else.

Appendix 2: Calculations

Many of these calculations are useful some of the time: understanding when to use them and how is equally important; they are included here as a reference.

Correlation: for Understanding, Anticipation and Prognostication of Economic Factors

Caution! Correlation does not imply causation. Just because two or more factors are co-incidental does not mean that there is not an unknown factor that causes this co-incidence. However, it is not always necessary to understand the nature of causation, it may suffice under many circumstances to simply be aware of the phenomenon.

Correlation is measured in terms of a positive or negative coefficient: a correlation of +1 or -1 indicates a 100% connection between co-incidental factors, either in a supportive or detrimental role. A 0 indicates a 0% or non-connection, a disconnection, between the factors. In other words, for non-zero coefficients, there is a high probability that the two factors will occur **simultaneously.**

Scientific method requires the analysis of one controlled factor at a time: though hundreds of factors may be analyzed, it is proper to examine how they impact each other one at a time.

This calculation requires understanding the co-variance of the factors: how much do they shift together in response to a controlled variable?

Though the mathematics requires some training in algebra, many computers will perform this calculation automatically using a correlation computation equation. In Google Sheets, or Microsoft Excel, this is convenient. For Google Sheets, input the two data sets, and then in a different cell type =CORREL([DATA SET 1],[DATA SET 2]) (using the columnular and cellular designation for each set). It really is that easy.

	A	B	C	D
1	=CORREL(B3:B14,C3:C14)			
2		Factor A	Factor B	
3	January	1	1	
4	February	1	2	
5	March	2	3	
6	April	3	4	
7	May	5	5	
8	June	8	6	
9	July	13	7	
10	August	21	8	
11	September	34	9	
12	October	55	10	
13	November	89	11	
14	December	144	12	
15				
16				
17				
18				
19				
20				
21				
22				
23				
24				
25				
26				
27				
28				
29				
30				
31				

fx =CORREL(B3:B14,C3:C14)

*Here, using Googlesheets, we calculate the correlation of a fibonacci sequence to a linear progression. The correlation comes to 0.834, indicating there is an 83.4% coincidence between the two sets of data: there is an 83.4% chance that when one increases, the other will do so **proportionately**, allowing a prediction of the next value: though we understand the next fibonacci number to be 233 (being the sum of 144 and 89), if we didn't, we would see that 144 is approximately 83.4% of 233 (it is actually 62%, but we are approximating in a prognostication based on limited data). The more data we get the better we can predict sequences of random and non-random data, and discover the connections between them. In fact, if we do add in another "month" of data, we learn that the correlation goes down to 81%, suggesting that our approximation of 83% is too high, and also there is a non-linear but progressive relationship between the numbers in the fibonacci sequence.*

Correlation is necessary to use in prognostication if the two data sets are offset by timing. While Factor A may not cause Factor B, if there is a high probability that the two factors coincide when Factor A occurs 1 month later, or 1 year later, or 1 hour later than Factor B - then it is possible to anticipate Factor A occuring within that time frame after Factor B.

	A	B	C
1	=CORREL(B4:B14,C4:C14)		
2		Factor A	Factor B
3	January		1
4	February	1	2
5	March	1	3
6	April	2	4
7	May	3	5
8	June	5	6
9	July	8	7
10	August	13	8
11	September	21	9
12	October	34	10
13	November	55	11
14	December	89	12
15	January	144	

fx =CORREL(B4:B14,C4:C14)

Here, we offset the data to allow a "delay" so that January's Factor A is aligned with February's Factor B, examining whether coincidence is increased: if it takes a month for Factor A to effect factor B we would see this correlation increase because what we observe in February for Factor B would have been caused in January by Factor A - or perhaps, whatever affected Factor A in January takes a month longer to affect Factor B.

Let's also examine this concept graphically.

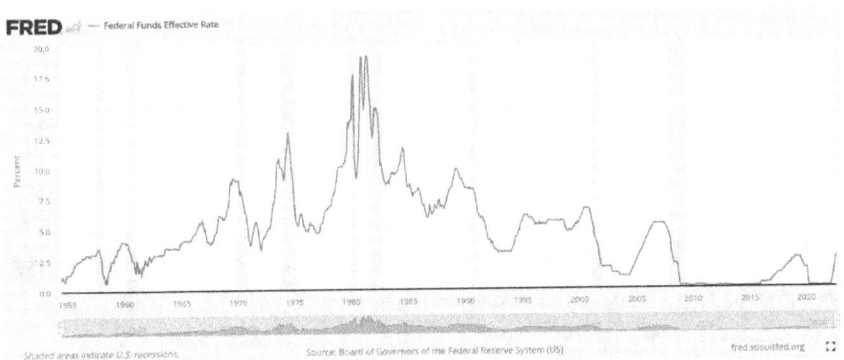

Above is the history of the Federal Funds Effective Rate from 1955 to 2022. Shaded areas indicate US recessions. Graphically, we can see that there is a co-incidence of the FFER decreasing during recessions: every recession has a reducing rate. However, we do not see a co-incidence of decreasing rates and recessions: the rate is sometimes reduced without a recession. Therefore, we may determine

- There is a predictive value of a recession and a diminishing FFER during that recession
- There is no predictive value of the FFER being reduced and a recession

Let's take this one step further. Is there any co-incidence between the FFER and the SP500 Index? Can the effects of changes in FFER predict SP500 values?

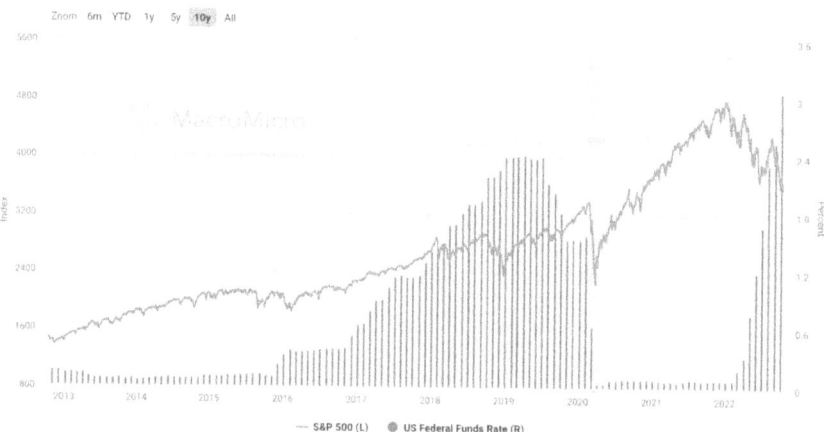

Looking at the last 10 years we see what is apparent over any period of time: there is no coincidence between the changes in the FFER and the SP500. Even if the rates of the FFER go up, or down, or stay constant, there is no immediate or subsequent change to the SP500. And, the reverse is true as well: changes to the SP500 do not coincide with changes to the FFER.

These tools of correlation and prognostication are even more effective when causation is known. For example, if we understand a supply chain, we can anticipate changes to the costs of raw materials will impact the overall costs of production down the line and ultimately the cost the consumer is paying. But, for example, how long does it take for a cost in oil to affect the cost of mining iron, or the cost of transporting food, or the price of shoes?

One limitation to this is that sometimes in non-competitive markets causation lies ultimately in those who control the price things are bought or sold, rather than by any natural market pressures. A grocery store may understand that fuel prices are rising and raise their prices in anticipation of these higher costs of business - or even attempt to gouge their customers, using fuel prices as an excuse (raising the prices higher than they need to, or more quickly). However, so long as the monopolist exhibits predictable behavior, and is not erratic or capricious in exercising their power, we may anticipate them anyway.

But one additional application of correlation is sometimes also permits a glimpse into the responses of individual companies within a sector of the economy, or different sectors: does one respond quicker or more severely than another to a similar factor, like rising fuel costs?

Standard Deviation: Understanding What Factors Warrant Correlative Analysis, Understanding Individual Companies and Sectors in an Economy

Calculating the standard deviation is important to understand whether what we are observing is significant, and how significant, permitting us to do away with irrelevance and focus on what is important.

The concepts of significance and relevance should be explored, as they are rooted in the theories of logic - which are advanced concepts, that may be adequately summarized and simplified through several premises:

1. There is truth
2. But what is true cannot be known with total certainty
3. What is not true can be known with certainty
4. These untruths are not necessarily falsehoods: what is not untrue is not true, it may simply be unknown
5. Because there are untruths that are both known and unknown, and so much of the truth is uncertain, we may develop a reasonable estimate of how certain we are that something is true.

By this we conclude: this coefficient of truth, our "certainty," or "confidence," of our knowledge of what is true suggests that **some facts complete our understanding of what is true more or less than others**: this is the significance of these facts.

Therefore, facts which are significant are relevant to our search for truth and deserve investigation and study, facts which are insignificant are irrelevant and cannot justify our inquiry: if understanding something will only increase our confidence or knowledge of what is true a microscopic amount, our efforts are better applied to discovering facts which will more greatly increase our confidence in what is true.

Thus do we calculate the standard deviation to understand whether what we are looking at is unusual, and whether it contributes significantly to our understanding of the whole: if what we examine is removed from the whole, by how much does our comprehension change?

If a company is very much standard within its sector or economy, then it is typical, and much can be gained in our understanding of the average by studying it. If, however, a company is unusual, atypical, non-standard - then its uniqueness presents opportunity to understand factors which are unusually at play, and better comprehend the role of these factors.

There are numerous ways to apply the standard deviation calculation: we may understand the relative weight of each company's contribution to the industry by comparing its output, profit, wealth, or other factors to the sector; we may compare sales data and understand if it is gaining or losing sales in significant proportion to other companies. The examples are endless and do not serve to further the basic understanding sought here.

Merely understand this: the tool is versatile, but the purpose is to tease from understanding what is the same and what is different to gain awareness of those factors warranting further study through correlative analysis. Put another way, in understanding if the company or sector is unique, and the amount by which it differs from other companies, and in what regard, we may apprehend by those differences and similarities awareness of factors perhaps worthy of our study.

To calculate the standard deviation of a data set using google sheets, you may utilize the function =STDEV([DATA SET]). This is meaningless without calculating the average from which the data deviates, use =AVERAGE([DATA SET]). Adding and subtracting one, two or even three standard deviations from the average will indicate, respectively, all the data that lies 68% outside the expected average (+/-1 standard deviation), 95% outside the expected average (+/-2 standard deviations), 99.5% outside the expected average (+/- 3 standard deviations), etc. This suggests how unusual or typical the data in question is: if 99.5% of data is unlike it, it is highly unusual and highly significant; if 68% of data is like it, it is not unusual and insignificant.

Unless you are trying to study what is average.

www.ingramcontent.com/pod-product-compliance
Lightning Source LLC
Chambersburg PA
CBHW070301220526
45465CB00004B/1698